I'M READY TO SAY YES!

Louise Smith

I'm Ready to Say Yes!
Copyright © 2010 by Kingdom Builders
Publications

All rights reserved. No part of this book may be reproduced or transmitted in any form or by any means without written permission from the author.

All Scripture inn this text is derived from the King James Version (KJV).

ISBN 978-1-467-59183-6
Library of Congress Control Number: 2013921849
Printed in USA

Dedication

Thank you for saying yes to the plan, will, and purpose of God for your life. Use your imagination, persistence, and faith to accomplish the good life. Be successful, and multiply.

Louise Smith

This book is dedicated to all people who would like to get a moral and righteous handle on life. There is a holistic way of living and getting the tools to do it are partly found in these words. God bless you and thank you for your quest. I am hopeful you will find help.

Preface

I am delighted to have been asked by Minister Louise Smith to be a part of this project. The reader of this book will recognize that Louise has attempted and succeeded in seven short chapters to provide practical instructions to anyone who desires to say yes to the will, plan, and purpose of God for their life. As you make your way through this book, you will see that it is a book written with words that anyone can read and understand.

This book will build one's faith in God who allows us free choice in all matters. As you read this book, you will discover that God is not an absolute monarch who demands blind obedience and the mere fact that we have the option of saying "yes"…or "no" to Him in the first place speaks volumes of His loving nature. This book will encourage love and trust in an everlasting God.

Minister Smith makes it clear in this book that God chooses plain, ordinary people like you and me and issues us all an invitation to a fuller, deeper, purposeful, and more meaningful life. He calls upon us to use the precious gifts He has given to us throughout our lives.

Minister Smith challenges the reader to see that we don't have to be perfect to say "yes" to God…and He doesn't expect us to be perfect after we say "yes" to Him. The good news is that He loves us as we are and loves us enough *not* to leave us as we are. As we say yes to God's salvation plan, will, and purpose for our lives, He helps us to become better than what we are.

The only thing required to say yes to God is faith. Saying yes to God is expressing confidence in His character. Saying yes to God is saying we trust the direction He will lead us. In saying yes to God, we are affirming that we believe He loves us and has our best interests at heart. Saying yes to God enables us to unite with God's purpose for our lives. For some, this book is a first step to saying yes to God, for others it's a reminder of the benefits of saying yes to Him. Now that you're ready, say yes!

Peace, Favor, and Blessings

Bishop Eric B. Morris, Pastor
Citadel of Hope Christian Ministries
Columbia, SC

Introduction

You've wanted to change your lifestyle, wanted to try something different, but just have not felt the "clean scene" or the "holy-rolly church scene." You have probably recognized that there is a higher power out there somewhere; a God; a strong presence, but you're pretty sure He's not in the mood to hear your prayers because you have not been living the best way or making good decisions about life. I'll bet you're thinking that if you were to pray, your prayers wouldn't reach the ceiling, let alone get to God. You've probably heard that erroneous quote, "God don't hear no sinner's prayer!" Now, if you really put credence to that, you would really consider how MUCH of a lie that is. How could we come to him with of hope of change, if He's not going to even lend an ear. If that were the case everybody in LIFE; to include the BIBLE guys would be defeated and doomed forever. So…If you were thinking in any of those directions; thinking this maybe your plight, then boy do I have an enlightenment for you! This is your *"gravy-boat"* news flash! Jesus only used "the church" referring to it as "my church" one time in all of His dissertations and sermons. He always spoke on the Kingdom of God or the Kingdom of Heaven. His Spirit and the Kingdom can be in YOU, Yup, YOU! How about that?!

There are five quick but continual steps of YES I'd like to share with you! If you're ready to say yes, it's as easy as saying GRACE! One, two, three, four, five...let's go! You cannot come clean to something you are not aware of. You're not likely to admit to something you're not privy to or can't testify of.

Your Mom and Dad can say for a certainty that you were born on such and such day and date, and what the climate was. Well, of course you were there; but you cannot attest to that because you have no recollection of that. You can't say that you were actually born a certain day or a certain time. You're just going on the knowledge and testimony of others. Now, you do have your own experiences of moments in life that no one can take away from your memory.

Jesus has His personal testimony of each person He created. He has given each of us the measure of faith (Romans 12:3), a hope and a future (Jeremiah 29:11b). He readily admits that we are made in His glorious image and likeness. Jesus also gives us the facts and truth about decisions made that do not honor what is right. Choosing life will empower you to make righteous decisions (Matt 6:33) and have all spiritual blessings (Ephesians 1:3).

Choosing death means the absolute opposite. Please know that death is the direct result of sin. God defined it with Adam, and a slew of other men and women in the Bible. The same holds true today. **Deuteronomy 30:19** says, *"I call heaven and earth to record this day against you, that I have set before you life and death, blessing and cursing: therefore choose life, that both thou and thy seed may live:"* You will live your life in the dim of doom and curses because you chose to follow a non-authentic and wicked way. Doing what is right will give you joy. That will make you happy. Thus, you will live long and then some—like eternally. How about FOREVER!

Psst! In case you've never heard this, we are eternal beings. Yes, that's right, you will live forever. Now, the choice of how you live forever will greatly depend on your own decision to live in one of two camps: the kingdom of light or the kingdom of darkness.

Now we are all God's creation, but we are not all His children. We have to have a REBIRTH and a whole new mindset of thinking and change. **(John 1:12, John 3:7, Romans 8:9, Romans 12:2)**

I could be wrong on this thought, but I think most children are afraid of the dark. So WHY would you choose dark over light; evil over good, the Devil over God? God has come to you to cut the light on and show you a whole new world (way) of thinking (living)!

God is pretty adamant when He said in **Romans 6:23**, *"For the wages of sin is DEATH,* *but the gift of God is ETERNAL LIFE through Jesus Christ our LORD.* " Life and death have their recompense. What life choice will you make, my friend? Will you choose to make wholesome decisions about everything concerning your living? Or will you choose the ways of the froward and experience the three deaths: spirit, soul, and body? If you live by the sword, you die by the sword, and continue your eternity in turmoil and torment. If you live a quiet and peaceable life; you will die with peace and continue your eternity in honor and happiness.

However, I'm not suggesting that you should have a suck-up, a "yes-man" or a "whatever you say Boss" mentality or spirit. I'd never imply that one should ever have adventure or take risks in life for his own life! That would be quite the same as being DEAD!

What I am saying is the wrong thing to do in life is to go about in life doing deliberate WRONG. Most of the human population have the understanding of what is right and what is wrong. Jesus went about just "DOING GOOD."

Things like speaking kind, being a help, encouraging, and other things that made a difference in another's life. We can ALL certainly choose to go in that direction.

Don't fight it, switch. Say "yes" to the great life!

Chapter One
Submission / Admission

Do you know what happens in traffic if you didn't yield to oncoming traffic? You'd probably get seriously hurt causing an accident or mortally wounding yourself or someone else. So you make a conscience decision to merge in or yield to another way for safety. Submission is not always a fun thing, but it can be very effective in your whole life scheme. Now, admitting that is a great place to start. Can you submit your thinking to a whole different perspective such as admitting that God made the Heaven and the earth? Everything you see came from God, and that you were made in His image. Everything that is seen, felt, heard, tasted and smelt comes from the direct imagination of a HOLY Being called Jehovah. If you can admit that God is THE SUPREME BEING OF THE UNIVERSE, and that there is no other God that creates, knows all, sees all, and is all powerful, then and only then will you have made your FIRST STEP! If you can admit from the absence of pride that you can't deliver yourself from yourself, that you need someone more smarter, wiser, powerful, and creative than yourself. Now you're surely on your way to an open door.

I must know that anything I seek after in this life is my search for something whole, true, constant, and loving. God is all of these things. It is not entirely in man alone, although there might be a measure of all of these in man, only GOD is infinite in wisdom, might, power, creativity and even honor.
I must confess that no other person, place or thing can complete me in my spirit but God and God alone.

Prayer:

God, I pray with a confessing knowledge that you are the God of Heaven and earth. I confess that I am made in Your image. I declare that you are everything that is good and right and true and holy. I say that I am nothing and that you are everything. I confess that even though I am made in your image, the first Adam caused sin into mankind and separated my spirit from your SPIRIT. I confess that I need you back in my life, so I can be whole, free, saved from the curse of sin and death, and delivered, in Jesus name, Amen.

I John 1:9 – *If we confess our sins, he is faithful and just to forgive us our sins (deeds) and to cleanse us from all unrighteousness.*

Chapter Two
The Trust Factor

Trust is the same as faith. When you go to sub sandwich or the chicken and barbeque joint, you trust that your present meal is going to be as good now as it was the last time you ate there. When you accelerate your car, you trust that you will make it to your destination without mechanical failure. God was so smart to give us faith. We all have it! A baby, who has no language, has faith. It starts to cry, and without fail, its needs will be met by feeding, changing, comforting, or entertaining. When you work on your job, you hope with confidence that you will get your remittance at the end of your work period. A child has that simple reliance on its parents; that all the gifts wanted for Christmas will be under the tree Christmas morning. You don't see words floating in the atmosphere after they have been spoken, but you hear them and respond to them. Faith is saying what you want, and expecting it to manifest or materialize with great confidence. Some people cannot trust what they do not see, only because their trust factor has been damaged due to someone's failure to keep their word or promise. It happened so much that anything which isn't tangible is deemed "not real". A small child with a missing parent in the home lacks trust. A person that was constantly violated physically, mentally, or sexually lacks trust. But I want to add: you can't see inside your body, but for a certainty, these things exist; water, pigment, layers of skin, mucus, organs, tissue, ligaments, cells, blood, bones even your germs. You can't literally see air, but it does exist. Without air or the organs in your body, you would not, could not live! Yes, you KNOW that you breathe by air, and that your body functions through the touch of God and heartbeat, blood, and brain getting the signals, but you still have to trust or believe, or have faith to rise up the next day and depend on God to let you live.

Having said all of that, I want you to trust this truth: God wants you to have the same faith

Jesus had when he healed the sick and raised the dead; the same faith God had to make the heavens and the earth and all that dwells in it, and all of the universe. Have the God kind of faith that caused the fig tree to dry up the day He spoke to it "NO MORE LIFE or fruit you will bear. Trust that God's SPIRIT will invade your human spirit and do regeneration inside you! His work is complete and GOOD. You will have the capacity to have peace, joy, love, compassion, stick-to-it-tive-ness with mercy and grace and all sufficiency because we have GOD! Trust that God wants to be your parent; your ABBA (Father), your protector. He is jealous of anyone's finite power to protect you. Believe that Jesus came to abolish the old way of death, hell, and destruction. Consider that Jesus came to give you a great life in great abundance. This means your entire self: spirit, soul, and body; mentally, emotionally, physically, naturally, spiritually, financially, and every other entity. Rely on God never to leave you in a desolate state. God is like air. He is always there and ever present.

Dear God, I trust that you know what is best for me, and that you came to give me a better way, the truth, and life. All of these are found in you and they are found in me. I believe that you was born, crucified, buried and rose again for my life to be abundant. I trust that you know me and hear my heart. I am a sinner doomed to a hell's eternity without you. I trust that you know what is best for me. You have not condemned me but have convicted me through the Cross. I am ready to lose the guilt and the shame. I trust you to help me change my life, in Jesus name, Amen.

Chapter Three
The Gift

Have you ever been handed a present and you say; "Nope, I don't want your gift." That would be quite inconsiderate, rude, or worse. It's just nice to be thought of. Well, Christ Jesus thought of you, while you were a sinner, he died for you so salvation would be available to you. **Romans 5:8** *God gave his love to us while we were sinners, He died for us.*

Can you imagine needing a vital organ to live? Then someone says, "I'll give you my organ so you can live. I will give you my life because I love you so much and I want you to experience the rest of your life whole." Now, you know your parents loves you unconditionally and would without fail come to the rescue, It could possibly happen of a sibling or your ace-coon-boon! But at the real time of need, who would want to chance it. These are select and rare situations that comes straight out of AGAPE and would not be the norm for everyone, or that it would happen all the time. But that's what our Brother; the First born of many brothers did in our stead. Neither you nor I were fit to live or fit to die, but He took our place on the cross to give us liberty, a hope, and a future again. WOW! What a love. What a gift!

It is Christmas Day. "Mas" means more in Spanish, so get Christ... and more of Christ; everyday starting today! Receive Christ the Spiritual Gift of life.

Prayer:

Thank you Father for making me your creation, and now I want to be your son. Thank you Jesus for dying for my sin (nature) and being raised from the dead, so that I too can rise from dead things! I confess that you raised Jesus from the dead with all power in His hands. Romans 10:8b –10, This is the word of faith which we preach: that if I confess with my mouth the Lord Jesus and shall believe in my heart that God has

raised him from the dead, I shall be saved. For with the heart man believes unto righteousness and with the mouth confession is made unto salvation. I confess that you have raised me from the dead. I have all power and authority to make great choices for the good life. I can have life in great abundance.

Glory to God, if you believe Christ, you have just received Christ's way of thinking and living. I pray this prayer in Jesus name, Amen.

Chapter Four
That's Good Enough to Share

That is news worth sharing with everyone. Don't assume everyone knows the GOSPEL or is not interested in the ABUNDANT LIFE of the GOSPEL. This is the same gospel that revolutionized your life, and it will do the same for a stranger, friend or relative.

Love, Work, Give, and Rest! These are the elements for a successful lifestyle. God gave you the ability to get wealth. So begin in your mind. Change your thinking for sharing. As you practice your Christianity, share the benefits of working (serving) for God. You can't go wrong. The Bible says we are the salt of the earth, so we have to make people thirsty for the Living Water. People are yearning for sugar and salt, bread wine, and meat. It's up to you to be a good taster, sweet smell or sound. The one way to give them the ingredients to life is to smile, show love by being kind, pray for one another and be a terror to the devil and his co-hoards by

NEVER allowing the enemy (you included) to turn you away from your dreams, goals, and desires. God has called you and only you to do an assignment that only you can do. It is profitable to you to get it done.

We all have a family, friends, comrades, peers, associates, co-workers, neighbors, church members, and even enemies. Everybody needs to know this great God and this great gospel! Get started today. Practice, Practice, Practice! Don't' be afraid or ashamed!

Prayer:

Lord, you are my protection and my direction in life. I love you so much that I will share your great gospel of what you did for me. You love me so much that you would do the same thing for the people I am around often. Thank you for the principle of each one reach one. Thank you for boldness to speak your word, and humility at the might. You are awesome to love us, bless us, heal us, comfort us, chastise us, and send us. I will never take your praise, glory, honor or even blame. I will be with you every day of my life. Give me people to share your love with today for my inheritance. He who wins souls is wise and you gave me the ministry of reconciliation. Thank you for the privilege and the opportunity to honor your character and to honor and live out my own new character. In Jesus name, Amen

I contribute to others lives, it makes me rich, abundantly supplied and without lack. I am ready to say yes to a peaceable lifestyle, a holy and wholesome resolve. People will see that I have changed because my whole outlook will change. Doing good keeps my mind and body healthy. Thank you for always wanting me to prosper and be in health as my mind will and intellect matures.

Chapter Five
Now I've Gotta Get Some New Reading Material

Well, I've been looking at television, on all the social media, renting movies, and spending time on the phone, but now I've gotta give all that stuff up, because I'm a Christian now, right? Friend there is a bit of truth to your question. While too much of anything is not good for you, I submit that you can enjoy the pleasures of great music, TV, internet surfing, and your favorite cinema. The Lord wants you to enjoy your life. Remember He wants you to HAVE LIFE MORE ABUNDANTLY. When the Lord did the work of salvation to your spirit, you were translated into the kingdom of His dear Son and into the marvelous light from darkness. There will always be a war between the spirit and the flesh. Galatians 5:17. Make a commitment to court (discover) your new life. In order to mimic someone, you must know those tones, words, the rise and fall of voices, outstanding gestures. Well, living the integrity and character of GOD, we must learn how Jesus did His life. Study. Look. Talk. Serenade. Fellowship. While you are learning your new nature, your old nature will contest your every decision. BUT, you have the righteous mind, the mind that was also in Christ Jesus. You will err, but your determination must be stronger to do what is right, righteous, holy, sacred, true, and lovely. You must be sound and sober (clear thinking) about all else. Your weapon is MIGHTY through GOD and your own imagination. Listen, you ALREADY KNOW WHAT IS RIGHT AND WHAT IS WRONG! Sin feels good, and has instant gratifications, but doing what is right will have a more lasting effect on you to the positive. SO let me challenge you to be sober about your life.

Your friend is NOT the accuser, the false speaker, the counterfeiter; he is the Devil. Learn what the Bible says, so you won't be tricked by what the enemy says. Then gain your balance.

You must know what's going on in the world. All Bible and no other reading materials will leave you in the dark about your life. While the news, weather and sports can't help you live a Godly lifestyle, it will keep you abreast of current events. You sway your entertainment away from things that will cause you to sin in your eyes, ears, and mind. Overeating, overspending are just as sinful as, sex before marriage and adultery, being a town drunk, druggie or street walker. You are probably asking that ancient old question, do I have to give up smoking and drinking and chasing after women, or looking for a man? No you don't have to give up any of these things to become a Christian. You aren't able anyway. You just come to the Lord, and He will help you. Through the work of Divine nature and your willingness to let your acts of sin go, it will happen. Now in order for this to happen, Jesus will have to be MORE than savior, He's gonna have to be LORD! There is nowhere in the Bible that tells you must give up tobacco, gambling, drinking swearing and fighting or even the style of clothes to wear. You may even go to Heaven doing it. (YOU WILL HOWEVER, GET THERE MUCH QUICKER THAN THOSE WHO DO NOT HAVE THESE DESTRUCTIVE HABITS). You see you still have choice in every matter. You may choose to live like a hellion until the day of Jesus Christ. You may reserve your rights all the way up to the fire and brimstone at the judgment seat of Christ. Guess what? God will reserve his judgment and justice too! But here is the guarantee: if you talk to God every day and every night admitting when things are difficult or thanking Him when you overcame an obstacle, read or listen to the love letters of His heart (B.I.B.L.E.) Basic instructions before leaving earth, you will win over your battles. You will find yourself not even wanting to do the things of the flesh that will destroy your spirit, will, mind, intellect, imagination and body. So go on, and live your life to the fullest.

Chapter Six
Rules of Engagement

Wish I could tell you that once you are righteous, your life will be alleviated from troubles, money problems, mean spirited people, but it ain't true, Friend. If the truth be told, it seems to get worse. But be of good cheer. That's the name of the game: Kill, Steal, and Destroy! The devil's job is to get you to get away from righteous living. If you have determination, a hope, some faith and love, these will definitely win over any and ALL devises the devil tries to bring in your path. You've just gotta know the rules of the game. Cast down imaginations that exhort fear and anything that doesn't promote wholesomeness. Replace those thoughts in your imagination with a prayer, scripture, song, or a confession to overcome the corrupt thought in your mind. Then you have the authority to use the name of JESUS for everything in life. His name is power. The devils are subject to THAT name. They are afraid of the name and the power. Finally, resist doing wrong, hearing wrong from within (your imagination, mind, will or intellect) or without (any other person, place or thing). Your will and power will cause the devil to flee from you. These are the rules of engagement.

Remember, there is NONE righteous no not one (Romans 3:10) and there is none that doeth good, no not one (Romans 3:12). You NOW have the Righteous ONE inside you, living in your soul and spirit. Access Him. Allow Christ's character to live inside your mind, soul, will, and human spirit.

Chapter Seven
Great Tip

No preacher man, no policeman, no song, no last experience will keep you or keep you from doing what you REALLY want to do. It is a matter of CHOICE. It is a matter of the heart.

Here is a true story about twins who were raised in the house by the same adults. One twin became a trifling drunk. He would drink day in and day out. He never owned a job, wife or children. One particular day while in the liquor store, the owner had a heart to heart with the man. Yes, he wanted to sell his product to everyone that comes in his store, but in his heart of hearts, he felt he needed to deter this man. So he said to him, "Man, why won't you stop drinking and get on a better path. You're killing yourself." The twin responded with a sort of hatred for himself for being in this out of control state, and for the owner of the liquor store for saying to him such a thing. Further he was perturbed for the store owner being present in his neighborhood with the store in the first place. His reply was, "Man I can't change. I want to, but my daddy was a drunk. This is all I know. I can do no better!" as he poured down another drink. Meanwhile his twin brother was named the head of a fortune 500 company. He landed another enormous account of the year and the office wanted to celebrate him for his accomplishments. They had a party for him with all types of beers, champagnes, booze and coolers. His co-workers were all throwing back the drinks. One of his associates came over with an imported beer in hand to get him involved more personally with the celebration and asked him, "Man, I was watching you. Congratulations on your account landing and your new promotion. Say man with all these Honeys and all this wine and booze, man you're not grabbing at none of it. I've never seen you drink. EVER! This is a big deal. You are the man. You landed the most important gig of this job. Man it's okay to get your man on!" The other twin replied, "Naw, Bruh. You've never seen me drink because I don't drink. In fact I will never drink! My daddy was a drunk." He never made it out of the prison of his mind. I must be level-headed and sober. Wisdom is the principal thing. In all my getting, I must get an understanding. I understand that drinking could destroy me."

Every decision belongs to you! Only you can sway you. Take responsibility for your actions. Practice doing what is right. Live a quiet and peaceable life. Success is yours. Joshua 1:8 - This book of the law shall not depart out of your mouth, and you shall meditate day and night that you may observe to do all that is written therein: for then you shall make your way prosperous, and you will have good success.

Welcome to your NOW, NEW abundant and eternal life. You Rejoice! Heaven rejoices. The Kingdom of God rejoices, as do we!

Please request prayer, invite us to coach you or share your testimony with us.

Minister Louise Smith
www.kingdombuilderspublications.com
kbpublications@outlook.com
toll-free 844-669-7180